KETO INSTANT POT COOKBOOK

Ketogenic Soup, Breakfast, Beef, Chicken, Pork, Turkey and Curry recipes for Instant Pot.

Table of Contents

Terms Of Use Agreement

Disclaimer

The author and the publisher have used their best efforts in preparing this book. The author and the publisher make no representation or warranties with respect to the accuracy, fitness, applicability, or completeness of the contents of this work and specifically disclaim all warranties, including without limitation warranties of fitness for a particular purpose. This work is sold with the understanding that author and the publisher is not engaged in rendering legal, or any other professional services.

The information contained in this book is strictly for educational purposes. Therefore, if you wish to apply ideas contained within this book, you are taking full responsibility for your actions. The author and the publisher disclaim any warranties (express or implied), merchantability, or fitness for any particular purpose. The Author and The publisher shall in no event be held responsible / liable to any party for any indirect, direct, special, punitive, incidental, or other consequential damages arising directly or indirectly from any use of this material, which is provided 'as is', and without warranties.

The author and the publisher do not warrant the performance, applicability, or effectiveness of any websites and other medias listed or linked to in this publication. All links are for informative purposes only and are not warranted for contents, accuracy, or any other implied or explicit purpose.

Introduction

Thank you for purchasing this Keto diet Cookbook that is full of delicious recipes for Instant Pot. I heard a statement saying that Ketogenic diet caused a revolution in dieting, and to be honest, I must agree with it. But I also believe that Instant Pot caused revolution within home cooking industry. And inside of this book you will find combinations of both; cooking keto recipes inside of your Instant Pot.

This publication doesn't contain directions for using the Instant Pot, or any tips and tricks. It seems to be common trend in these days to include 20 pages of explanations such as; what instant pot is and what each button means ... etc. I believe that everything is pretty well explained in user manual that came with your pot. Therefore main focus of this book is on actual recipes.

As much as I didn't want to turn this book into another user manual for the Instant Pot, I have to dedicate little bit of space to ketogenic diet.

Is the keto diet, another typical fad diet? Actually, it's been around for a while now, and people are getting pretty good results from it. So what exactly keto diet is?

Well, most of these fad diets you find simply tells you to eat this certain type of food and avoid those certain type of food and voila, you're on your way to losing a hundred pounds!

Of course, a lot of them don't really work. What's special about the keto diet, short for ketogenic, is that it changes how your body feels, and most importantly, how your body uses energy by placing you into a state known as ketosis. And this is where all the magic happens. In ketosis, your body starts utilizing substances known as ketone bodies, which are produced by the breakdown of your body fat triglycerides.

Quick science, first understand that your body loves glucose. If it has glucose on hand, it's going to use that first for energy. In a keto diet, the amount of carbohydrates you consume goes down, therefore, the amount of glucose goes down, too. In order to combat this, your body uses stored glucose in the form of glycogen, but then that's going to run out as well. The next step is to convert a substance known as oxaloacetate in the liver into glucose. At the same time this is happening, your body is breaking down your fat into free fatty acids and sending it to your liver to metabolize another important substance known as acetyl CoA. Acetyl CoA is then placed into the Krebs cycle in the liver cells to produce energy. But it can't do that right now. Remember that oxaloacetate that was being broken down into glucose? Well, oxaloacetate is also needed for the Krebs cycle to function.

Now your liver has all of these acetyl CoA lying around so it decides to break it down into two substances called acetoacetate and beta-hydroxybutyrate, which are known as ketone bodies. It sends them into the bloodstream where other body cells pick them up, convert the ketone bodies back into acetyl-CoA, into Krebs cycle, and energy is produced! This is also really good news for your brain, since even though your brain loves glucose too, it can function on ketone bodies as well. In fact, ketone bodies provide more energy per gram for the brain versus glucose, so win-win for your mental capacity!

Now so far, everything sounds good. Your body no longer relies heavily on carbohydrates, it burns a lot of fat, and your brain functions pretty well. But of course, there's always a catch, a number of catches in this case. Studies show that power output decreases in cases where maximum intensity is required. This makes sense because the breakdown of glucose via glycolysis, plays a crucial role in providing immediate energy for your body.

With no glucose and glycogen in your body, intense workouts become a lot harder. And the lack of glycogen also affects muscle growth, since there is a strong positive connection between glycogen availability and protein synthesis. Take the glycogen away, and the process slows down. Oh, and there's the keto flu, something that happens when your body starts transitioning off of carbs and rely more heavily on ketone bodies. The "keto flu," which isn't an actual flu, contains symptoms such as headaches, fatigue, coughing, nausea, and even upset stomach. The positive note, though, is that it passes quite quickly and won't come back again unless you come out of ketosis.

The keto diet is also very food restrictive. A conventional diet has you eating roughly 20% fat, 30% protein, and 60% carbs. The keto diet, on the other hand, shifts you all the way to 70% fat, 25% protein, and 5% carbs, or below 30 grams. That's a huge change that some people just cannot do. Cutting out so many carbs is easier said than done. This is a huge battle itself, and a lot of times, a losing battle. But even with the drawbacks, people still advocate for it. And the reason that's the case can be summed up from this study in 2004 from the Annals of Internal Medicine: "a low-carbohydrate diet (such as a keto diet), had better participant retention" compared to a low-fat diet. That is saying, even with all the drawbacks, individuals on a keto diet find it much easier to stick to this kind of diet. This is because, with so much more fat and protein-dense foods, your satiety, or fullness level, goes up much faster. A 200 calorie chicken breast or 200 calories worth of green leafy vegetables, will make you feel more full than say a 200 calorie, carb-heavy pasta. But even if this is the case, a calorie is still a calorie. Yes, protein and fat calories will make you feel more full, but it won't help you lose weight if you're still eating more calories than you burn.

So is the keto diet worth it? Well, it all comes down to, "It depends." If you're someone who struggles a lot with feeling full whenever you go on a weight loss diet, then yes, the keto diet might help you battle those feeding frenzies. Just remember those drawbacks that will occur, and at the end of the day, it still comes down to calories in versus calories out.

Soup Recipes

Cauliflower Soup with a Twist

Serves: 6

Preps Time: 15 min

Cooking Time: 60 min

Ingredients:

- 1 tbsp olive oil
- 1 large yellow onion, diced
- 2 cloves garlic, minced
- 1 head cauliflower, coarsely chopped
- 1 green bell pepper, chopped
- 1 tbsp onion powder
- 32 oz of chicken stock
- 2 cups Cheddar cheese, shredded
- 6 slices cooked turkey bacon, diced
- 1 tbsp Dijon mustard
- hot pepper sauce to taste
- salt and black pepper, to taste

Direction:

1. Turn on your Instant Pot and choose the Saute function.
2. Add olive oil, onion, and garlic; cook until browned, which should take about 3 minutes.
3. Add cauliflower, green bell pepper, onion powder, salt, and pepper.
4. Add chicken stock.
5. Close and lock the lid. Press Soup function and set timer for 15 minutes.
6. Allow around 15 minutes to pressure up.
7. Release pressure according to manufacturer's instructions using quick-release. Should take about 5 minutes.
8. Unlock and remove lid. Add Cheddar cheese, turkey bacon, dijon mustard, and hot sauce.

9. Reselect Saute function and continue cooking until bubbly. It will take approximately 5 minutes.
10. Enjoy!

Hot Chicken Soup

Serves: 4

Preps Time: 15 min

Cooking Time: 30 min

Ingredients:

- 1 tbsp extra virgin olive oil
- 1 large yellow onion, diced
- 3 cloves garlic, minced
- 1 large red bell pepper, diced
- 1 large jalapeño, minced
- 240 oz tomato sauce, sugar-free
- 1 tbsp chili powder
- 1 tbsp chipotle pepper in adobo sauce
- 2 tsp ground cumin
- 1 tsp garlic powder
- 1 tsp onion powder
- 1 tsp white wine vinegar

- 1 tsp salt
- ½ tsp oregano
- 3 cups chicken stock
- 1 lb chicken breasts

Toppings

- avocado, diced
- jalapeno peppers, sliced

Direction:

1. Drizzle your Instant Pot with the olive oil and choose Sauté setting.
2. Add the onion, garlic, bell pepper, and jalapeño pepper.
3. Cook until soft. It will take approximately 3-4 minutes.
4. In a small bowl, mix together the tomato sauce, vinegar, chipotle chili, and spices. Pour the mixture into your Instant Pot.

5. Add the stock and chicken. Stir and cover with the lid.
6. Reset your Instant Pot to Manual high pressure and cook for 20 minutes.
7. Release the pressure.
8. Remove the chicken and shred it up. Place back into the pot and stir properly.
9. Top with desired toppings before serving.
10. Enjoy!

Mediterranean Taco Soup

Serves: 8

Preps Time: 10 min

Cooking Time: 10 min

Ingredients:

- 2 pounds ground beef
- 1 tbsp onion flakes
- 4 cloves garlic, minced
- 2 tbsps chili powder
- 2 tsp cumin
- 20 oz diced tomatoes with chilis
- 32 oz beef stock
- 8 oz cream cheese
- 1/2 cup heavy cream
- salt & pepper to taste

Direction

1. Add ground beef into your Instant Pot and brown it using sauté setting.
2. Drain excess grease if needed.
3. Add onion flakes, garlic, chili powder, cumin, diced tomatoes with chili, beef broth, and salt & pepper.
4. Cover your Instant Pot and cook for 5 minutes using soup setting.
5. After 5 minutes depressurize for 10 minutes.
6. Open vent valve and remove the lid.
7. Add cream cheese and cheese.
8. Enjoy!

Grans Veggie Soup

Serves: 12

Preps Time: 10 min

Cooking Time: 100 min

Ingredients:

- 1 large turnip, cubed
- 1 small onion, chopped
- 6 stalks celery, chopped
- 1 medium carrot chopped
- 15 oz pumpkin puree
- 1 pound green beans frozen or fresh
- 64 oz chicken stock
- 2 cups water
- 1 tbsp fresh basil, chopped
- 1/4 tsp thyme leaves
- 1/8 tsp sage, rubbed

- 1 pound fresh or frozen spinach leaves, chopped
- salt to taste

Direction:

1. Place all ingredients except spinach into your Instant Pot.
2. Cover and set the pot for 10 minutes - high pressure.
3. Once finished, allow 10 natural minutes to release pressure.
4. Open cover and stir in spinach.
5. Cover for 5 minutes.
6. Enjoy!

Indian Meat Stock

Serves: 6

Preps Time: 10 min

Cooking Time: 130 min

Ingredients:

- 1 chicken carcass
- 2 carrots, cut in chunks
- 1 cup chopped celery
- 1 tbsp apple cider vinegar
- 2 tsp ground turmeric
- 3 cloves garlic, minced
- 1 tsp fresh ginger,minced
- 4 cups warm water

Direction:

1. Combine chicken carcass, carrots, celery, vinegar, turmeric, garlic,ginger and place into your Instant Pot.
2. Add enough water to cover bones and vegetables in the pot.
3. Close and lock the lid. Select Manual function and set timer for 120 minutes.
4. Allow 10 to 15 minutes for pressure to build.
5. Release pressure using the natural-release method according to manufacturer's instructions. It should take 10 to 40 minutes.
6. Unlock and remove lid.
7. Cool it down for 10 minutes and strain.
8. Enjoy!

Ham and Cauliflower Soup

Serves: 8

Preps Time: 10 min

Cooking Time: 60 min

Ingredients:

- 3 tbsps olive oil
- 1/2 yellow onion, chopped
- 3 cloves garlic, sliced
- 1 ham bone with cca 3 cups of ham still attached
- 4 cups chicken stock
- 1 head of cauliflower, cut into small florets
- 1 cup heavy cream
- 1 cup white cheddar, shredded
- 1 cup sour cream
- 1/2 cup green onions, sliced
- salt and black pepper to taste

Direction:

1. Set your Instant Pot to sauté and add olive oil. Once olive oil is heated, add onions and garlic. Season with salt and pepper.
2. Stir and cook for about 2 minutes, until garlic becomes fragrant. Add in ham bone and stock. Turn off the heat.
3. Place on lid and set valve to sealing. Cook on high pressure and set the timer to 50 minutes.
4. Perform a quick release of pressure and allow button to drop on lid.
5. Remove ham bone and shred the meat off the bone.
6. Roughly chop the ham and return it to the pot.
7. Add cauliflower florets and heavy cream.
8. Taste and season the soup with salt and pepper if needed.

9. Cover with lid, set valve to sealing, and cook on high pressure for 5 minutes.
10. Quick release of pressure and allow button to drop on lid.
11. Stir in shredded cheddar.
12. Top each serving with sour cream and sprinkle with green onions.
13. Enjoy!

Chicken and Rice Soup

Serves: 6

Preps Time: 5 min

Cooking Time: 20 min

Ingredients:

- 1 cup onion, diced
- 1 cup celery, diced
- 1 cup carrots, diced
- 1 tbsp olive oil
- 3 chicken breast, cubed
- 48 oz chicken stock
- 1 box Uncle Ben's quick cooking wild rice
- ¼ tsp rosemary
- 1 tbsp parsley
- 1 tsp poultry seasoning
- 1 tsp garlic, minced
- ½ tsp Italian seasoning

- 1 tsp salt
- 1 tsp pepper

Direction:

1. Turn on your Instant Pot and choose the SAUTE function.
2. Add olive oil, onions, celery and carrots.
3. Leave it to saute for approximately 5 minutes.
4. Add 1 cup of chicken stock and stear.
5. Add cubed chicken, the seasoning packet from the wild rice, rice, 3½ cups chicken stock, and remaining seasoning.
6. Cover the lid and select MANUAL option on tour Instant Pot.
7. Set timer for 6 minutes.
8. Allow the pressure to build up. Usually takes about 3 minutes.
9. Once the time is up, use natural pressure release.

10. Open the lid and shred the chicken cubes with the fork.
11. Once again set your Instant Pot to SAUTE.
12. Pour in remaining chicken stock to reach desired consistency.
13. Boil the soup and switch Instant Pot off.
14. Enjoy!

Ham and Broccoli Soup

Serves: 6

Preps Time: 10 min

Cooking Time: 20 min

Ingredients:

- 2 tbsp coconut oil
- 3 leeks, white parts only - roughly chopped
- 2 shallots, roughly chopped
- 1 tbsp curry powder
- 1 ½ lb broccoli, chopped into uniform florets
- ¼ cup apple, peeled and diced
- 4 cups chicken stock
- 1 cup full-fat coconut milk
- 1/2 cup kalua Pork, crisped
- salt and black pepper to taste

- chives for garnish

Direction:

1. Turn on your Instant Pot and choose the SAUTE function.
2. Leave to heat up and add coconut oil, followed by leeks, shallots, curry powder and salt.
3. Cook while stirring for 5 minutes.
4. Add broccoli, apple and stir.
5. Add chicken stock.
6. Press the CANCEL/KEEP WARM" button on your Instant Pot.
7. Set the timer to 5 minutes and high pressure.
8. Once the time is up turn off the the Instant Pot and release the pressure manually.
9. Blitz the soup.

10. Add the coconut milk and season with salt and pepper.
11. Enjoy!

Mexican Chicken Soup

Serves: 4

Preps Time: 15 min

Cooking Time: min

Ingredients:

- 2 chicken breasts
- 14.5 oz chicken stock
- 28 oz mild enchilada sauce
- 14.5 oz diced tomatoes
- 4.5 oz mild green chiles, chopped
- 15 oz black beans, drained
- 2 cups corn, frozen

Optional Toppings

- Mexican cheese
- Tortilla strips
- Sour Cream

Direction:

1. Turn on your Instant pot and add stock, enchilada sauce, tomatoes, and chiles. Stir to combine.
2. Add chicken breasts and close the lid.
3. Choose High Pressure and set the timer to 5 minutes.
4. Once the time is up leave it for 10 minutes before performing a quick pressure release.
5. Take chicken breasts out from the soup and shred.
6. Return shredded chicken into the pot.
7. Add black beans and corn. Stir.
8. Choose the SIMER option to bring the soup back to a boil, stirring occasionally.
9. Serve topped with your favourite topping.
10. Enjoy!

Hot and Creamy Chicken Soup

Serves: 8

Preps Time: 5 min

Cooking Time: 25 min

Ingredients:

- 1 chicken breasts, cubed
- 3 tbsps butter
- 2 garlic cloves, minced
- 1/2 onion, chopped
- 1/2 green pepper, chopped
- 2 jalapenos, seeded - chopped
- 1/2 lb bacon, cooked - crumbled
- 6 oz cream cheese
- 3 cups chicken stock
- 1/2 cup heavy whipping cream
- 1/4 tsp paprika
- 1 tsp cumin

- 3/4 cup Monterey Jack Cheese
- 3/4 cup cheddar cheese
- 1/2 tsp xanthan gum
- salt and black pepper to taste

Direction:

1. Turn on your Instant Pot and choose the SAUTE function.
2. Add butter, onions, green peppers, jalapenos, and seasoning.
3. Saute for 5 minutes with the lid open.
4. Add cream cheese, stock, and chicken.
5. Close the lid and choose MANUAL option.
6. Set the timer to 15 minutes. Alove pressure to build up.
7. Once the time is up leave it for 5 minutes before performing a quick pressure release.
8. Choose SAUTE option on your Instant Pot.
9. Remove and shred the chicken breast.

10. Return shredded chicken back to the pot.
11. Add heavy whipping cream, cheeses, and bacon.
12. Saute and stir until the cheeses melt.
13. Sprinkle xanthan gum and simmer until you will reach desired consistency.
14. Serve topped with your favourite topping.
15. Enjoy!

Breakfast and Brunch

Caribbean Porridge

Serves: 6

Preps Time: 5 min

Cooking Time: 10 min

Ingredients:

- 1 cup unsweetened coconut, dried
- 2 cups coconut milk
- 2 cups water
- 1/4 cup coconut flour
- 1/4 cup psyllium husks
- 1 tsp vanilla extract
- 1/2 tsp cinnamon
- 1/4 tsp nutmeg
- 30 drops of stevia liquid
- 20 drops of monk fruit liquid

Direction:

1. Toast coconut in your Instant Pot until golden using sauté setting. Do not to burn!
2. Stir in water and coconut milk.
3. Cover the lid and set high pressure. Timer should be set to zero.
4. Once time is up, preform quick pressure release.
5. Open the lid and add the remaining ingredients.
6. Stir and serve.
7. Enjoy!

Dairy Free Yogurt

Serves: 6

Preps Time: 5 min

Cooking Time: 18 hrs

Ingredients:

2 cans coconut cream

4 capsules probiotic

Direction:

1. Start with pouring coconut cream into your Instant Pot.
2. Cover with the lid,and choose Yogurt setting.
3. Set to BOIL by using ADJUST button on the pots control panel.
4. Alarm will notify you once the boil temperature is reached. Open the lid and

add the powder from the probiotic capsules into the pot.

5. Stir using a whisk.
6. Cover with the lid and press the YOGURT button again.
7. Set the culture time to 18 hours.
8. Once finished, open the lid.
9. Pour it into a glass container, cover and let it chill for a day in the fridge.

Breakfast Boiled Eggs

Serves: 4

Preps Time: 1 min

Cooking Time: 4 min

Ingredients:

- 12 large eggs
- 1 cup water

Direction:

1. Insert the wire rack to the bottom of your Instant Pot.
2. Pour in 1 cup of water.
3. Gently place the raw eggs on the rack.
4. Close the lid, and make sure that the valve is closed.
5. Press the MANUAL button and set the time to 4 minutes

6. Cook on HIGH PRESSURE
7. Once the time is up, press CANCEL button and release the pressure.
8. Cool the eggs down in cold water.
9. Enjoy!

Mini Bacon Egg Bites

Serves: 8

Preps Time: 10 min

Cooking Time: 22 min

Ingredients:

- 4 eggs
- 1/4 cup egg whites
- 4 slices bacon, cooked - crumbled
- 1/2 cup reduced-fat cottage cheese
- 1/4 cup heavy whipping cream
- 1/2 red pepper, chopped
- 1/2 green pepper, chopped
- 1 cup red onion, chopped
- 1 cup gouda cheese, shredded
- 1 cup water
- salt and black pepper to taste

Direction:

1. Blend together eggs, egg whites, cottage cheese, whipping cream, shredded cheese, salt and pepper.
2. Turn on your Instant Pot and pour in 1 cup of water. Add the trivet which should come with your Instant Pot.
3. Place the baby-food container into the Pot.
4. Spoon the egg mixture into each of the compartments of the baby-food container.
5. Add chopped peppers, onions, and bacon on the top.
6. Cover baby food container with its lid.
7. Cover the lid of your Instant Pot.
8. Choose STEAM option and set the timer to 12 minutes.
9. Once the time is up perform natural steam release.
10. Remove baby food container container from the pot.

11. Allow to cool for 3 minutes.
12. Remove the bites from container and serve.
13. Enjoy!

Keto Souffle

Serves: 6

Preps Time: 10 min

cooking Time: 25 min

Ingredients:

- 1 head cauliflower
- 2 eggs
- 2 tbls cream
- 2 oz cream cheese
- 1/2 cup sour cream
- 1/2 cup asiago cheese
- 1 cup mild cheddar cheese
- 1/4 cup chives
- 2 tbsp butter, soft
- 6 rushes bacon, cooked, crumbled

Direction:

1. Add eggs, cream, cream cheese, sour cream, asiago and cheddar into the blender and blend until smooth and frothy.
2. Add cauliflower and continue to blend for about 10 seconds until chunky.
3. Add the chives and butter. Blend for another 5 seconds.
4. Pour the mixture into casserole dish that fits your Instant Pot.
5. Turn on the pot and add 1 cup of water. Insert the trivet into the pot.
6. Carefully place casserole dish onto trivet.
7. Close the lid and make sure that the pressure valve is on seal.
8. Change settings to MANUAL and choose HIGH PRESSURE.
9. Set the timer to 10 minutes.
10. Once the time is up perform quick pressure release.

11. Sprinkle with crumbled bacon and serve.
12. Enjoy!

Vanilla Rice Pudding

Serves: 2

Preps Time: 5 min

cooking Time: 60 min

Ingredients:

- 2/3 cup uncooked rice
- 4 cup milk
- 1/4 cup sugar
- 1 tsp vanilla extract

Direction:

1. Turn on your Instant Pot.
2. Add the rice and milk in the rice cooking bowl and stir to combine.
3. Close the lid and choose PORRIDGE option.
4. Once the time is up, open the lid.

5. Add the sugar and vanilla extract.
6. Stir well to combine.
7. Close the lid and reset for a second Porridge cycle.
8. Stir every 15 minutes until the desired consistency is reached.
9. Remember that the rice pudding will thicken as it cools down.
10. Serve and enjoy!

Beef Recipes

Country Chili

Serves: 4

Preps Time: 15 min

Cooking Time: 55 min

Ingredients:

- 1 1/4 lb ground beef
- 1/4 large onion, chopped
- 1 cup beef stock
- 4 cloves garlic, minced
- 15 oz diced tomatoes, liquid included
- 3 oz tomato paste
- 2 oz green chiles, with liquid
- 1 tbsp worcestershire sauce
- 1/8 cup chili powder
- 1 tbsp cumin
- 1/2 tbsp dried oregano
- 1 tsp salt

- 1/2 tsp black pepper
- 2 bay leafs

Direction:

1. Place chopped onion into your Instant Pot. Choose the SAUTE option and cook until translucent. Usually it takes 5-7 minutes. Do not cover with the lid.
2. Add the garlic and cook for another minute.
3. Add the ground beef. Cook for 8-10 minutes, until browned.
4. Add remaining ingredients, except bay leaf, and stir properly.
5. Now add bay leafs and close the lid.
6. Press KEEP WARM/CANCEL button to stop the saute cycle.
7. Select the MEAT/STEW option and pressure cook for 35 minutes.
8. Use the natural release of pressure.

9. Remove bay leafs and serve.
10. Enjoy!

Spicy Steak with Lime

Serves: 4

Preps Time: 5 min

cooking Time: 15 min

Ingredients:

- 2 lb fajita steak, cubed
- 1 tbsp of water
- 1 tsp garlic, minced
- 1 tbsp of EVOO
- 2 tsp of lime juice
- 1/2 tsp chili powder
- 1/2 tsp sea salt
- 1/2 tsp cracked pepper
- 1 tsp of cholula
- 2-3 avocado, diced

Direction:

1. Turn on your Instant Pot and select SAUTE option.
2. Pour in the olive oil and allow to heat up.
3. Add garlic and saute until golden.
4. Add all remaining ingredients except avocado
5. Stir well.
6. Close the lid and make sure that the pressure valve is on seal.
7. Change settings to MANUAL and choose HIGH PRESSURE.
8. Set the timer to 10 minutes.
9. Once the time is up perform quick pressure release.
10. Open the lid and change settings to SAUTE
11. Shred the meat inside the pot with the fork.
12. Saute until half of the liquid is reduced.
13. Serve with diced avocado.

14. Enjoy!

Mexican Beef Tacos

Serves: 4

Preps Time: 15 min

cooking Time: 60 min

Ingredients:

1 onion, chopped

2 tbsp olive oil

1 tsp. ground cumin

1 tsp. chili powder

2 lb flank steaks, trimmed, medium cubes

1 1/2 cup salsa

8 small taco-size lo carb flour tortillas

spicy Mexican slaw

limes for garnish

green tabasco sauce for serving

Direction:

1. Turn on your Instant Pot and select SAUTE option.
2. Pour in the olive oil and allow to heat up.
3. Add the onions and saute for 2-3 minutes.
4. Add the ground cumin and chili powder.
5. Continue to saute for another minute.
6. Add the meat and salsa.
7. Close the lid and make sure that the pressure valve is on seal.
8. Change settings to MANUAL and choose HIGH PRESSURE.
9. Set the timer to 45 minutes.
10. Once the time is up perform quick pressure release.
11. Scoop out the meat
12. Change the settings to SAUTE and reduce the liquid until you will reach desired consistency.

13. Shred the meat with the fork and return back to cooker.
14. Saute for 5 minutes stirring occasionally.
15. Heat up tortillas in a dry frying pan.
16. Serve on the top of tortilla with the slaw and green tabasco.
17. Garnish with lime.
18. Enjoy!

Tasty Beef Meatloaf

Serves: 4

Preps Time: 5 min

cooking Time: 35 min

Ingredients:

- 2 lb ground beef, grass fed
- 1 ¼ cup fire roasted salsa, divided
- 1 tsp cumin
- 1 tsp garlic powder
- 1 tsp chili powder
- 1 tsp paprika
- 1 tsp onion powder
- 1 tsp sea salt
- 1 tsp black pepper
- 1 yellow onion, diced
- 1 egg, pastured
- 1/4 cup tapioca starch

- 1 tbsp olive oil

Direction:

1. Turn on your Instant Pot and select SAUTE option.
2. Pour a cup of water into the Instant Pot.
3. In the separate bowl, mix all ingredients together. Keep 1/4 cup of the salsa aside.
4. Form the loaf from prepared mixture.
5. With the spoon, place 1/4 cup of remaining salsa on top of your meatloaf.
6. Wrap the loaf tightly to the foil.
7. Place wrapped meatloaf on the trivet.
8. Close the lid and make sure that the pressure valve is on seal.
9. Change settings to MANUAL and choose HIGH PRESSURE.
10. Set the timer to 35 minutes.
11. Once the time is up perform quick pressure release.

12. Open the lid and remove the loaf.
13. Serve with fresh cilantro sprigs.
14. Enjoy!

Indian Beef Roast

Serves: 4

Preps Time: 10 min

cooking Time: 40 min

Ingredients:

- 1 chuck roast, boneless
- 3 cloves garlic, crushed
- 2 tbsp fresh ginger, peeled and chopped
- 1 tsp orange extract
- 1/4 cup fish sauce, sugar free
- 2 tbsp granulated sugar substitute
- 1 tsp red pepper flakes, crushed
- 1/2 cup water
- 1 tbsp orange zest
- 1 tsp red wine vinegar

Sauce:

1/4 cup sugar free mayonnaise

1 tsp Sriracha hot sauce

1 tsp granulated sugar substitute

1/2 tsp fresh orange zest

Direction:

Roast Meat:

1. Turn on your Instant Pot and select MANUAL option.
2. Add the meat, garlic, ginger, orange extract, fish sauce, 1 tsp sweetener, red pepper flakes, and water into the pot.
3. Close the lid and make sure that the pressure valve is on seal.
4. Choose HIGH PRESSURE and set the timer to 35 minutes.
5. Once the time is up perform quick pressure release.
6. Change the setting to SAUTE.
7. Stir in the orange zest, 1 tsp sweetener, and red wine vinegar.

8. Saute for 5 minutes.
9. Serve with your favourite side dish.
10. Enjoy!

Sauce:

1. In a small bowl, mix together all of the sauce ingredients until smooth.

Ground Beef Goulash

Serves: 6

Preps Time: 15 min

cooking Time: 35 min

Ingredients:

- 2 lb lean ground beef
- 3 tsp olive oil, divided 2 -1
- 1 red bell pepper, seeded, short strips
- 1 onion, short strips
- 1 tsp garlic, minced
- 2 tsp sweet paprika
- 1/2 tsp hot paprika
- 4 cup beef stock
- 2 cans diced tomatoes

Direction:

1. Turn on your Instant Pot and select SAUTE option.
2. Pour in 2 tbsp of the olive oil and allow to heat up.
3. Add the ground beef and sautre for 7 minutes until browned.
4. Take the meat out of the pot and set aside.
5. Pour remaining 1 tsp of olive oil into the pot.
6. Add the onions and peppers.
7. Saute for 4 minutes.
8. Add garlic, sweet paprika, and hot paprika.
9. Saute for 3 stirring occasionally.
10. Add the stock, diced tomatoes, and browned beef.
11. Close the lid and make sure that the pressure valve is on seal.
12. Change settings to SOUP and set the timer to 15 minutes.

13. Once the time is up perform natural pressure release for 5 minutes and then quick pressure release.
14. Serve and enjoy!

Tasty Beef and Cabbage

Serves: 10

Preps Time: 15 min

cooking Time: 75 min

Ingredients:

- 4 lb corned beef brisket
- 6 cups water
- 2 tsp black peppercorns
- 4 cloves garlic
- 2 tsp dried mustard
- 1 head cabbage, cut into wedges
- 2 onions, sliced
- 4 carrots, sliced into thirds
- 4 celery stalks, chopped

Direction:

1. Turn on your Instant Pot and select MEAT/STEW option.

2. Place beef brisket into the pot.
3. Add the water and all spices.
4. Set the timer to 60 minutes.
5. Once the time is up perform natural pressure release.
6. Open the lid and press the SOUP button.
7. Take the meat out of the pot and set aside.
8. Add the vegetables to the pot and set the timer to 15 minutes.
9. Once the time is up perform quick pressure release.
10. Open the lid and return the meat back to the pot.
11. Serve and enjoy!

Royal Beef

Serves: 6

Preps Time: 5 min

cooking Time: 55 min

Ingredients:

- 3 lbs chuck roast
- 3 cloves garlic, thinly sliced
- 1 tbsp oil
- 1 tsp salt
- 1/2 tsp pepper
- 1/2 tsp rosemary
- 1 tbsp butter
- 1/2 tsp thyme
- 1/4 cup balsamic vinegar
- 1 cup beef stock

Direction:

1. With the sharp knife pierce the meat evenly all over and insert garlic into each whole.
2. In the separate bowl, combine the salt, pepper, rosemary and thyme.
3. Rub prepared mixture all over the roast beef.
4. Turn on your Instant Pot and select SAUTE option.
5. Pour in the olive oil and allow to heat up.
6. Add the beef roast to the pot and brown for 5 minutes on each side.
7. Take the meat out of the pot.
8. Add the butter, balsamic vinegar and stock.
9. Deglaze the pot by scraping up the browned bits and mixing with the liquid.
10. Insert the roast back in the pot.

11. Close the lid and make sure that the pressure valve is on seal.
12. Change settings to MANUAL and choose HIGH PRESSURE.
13. Set the timer to 40 minutes.
14. Once the time is up perform quick pressure release.
15. Open the lid and serve.
16. Enjoy!

Beef Lasagna

Serves: 8

Preps Time: 10 min

cooking Time: 25 min

Ingredients:

- 1 lb ground beef
- 1 tbsp olive oil
- 2 cloves garlic, minced
- 1 onion
- 1 cup water
- 1 1/2 cup ricotta cheese
- 1/2 cup parmesan cheese
- 1 egg
- 25 oz marinara sauce
- 8 oz mozzarella cheese, sliced

Direction:

1. Turn on your Instant Pot and select SAUTE option.
2. Pour in the olive oil and allow to heat up.
3. Add the ground beef, garlic and onion.
4. Saute for 5 minutes until browned.
5. In separate bowl, mix together the ricotta cheese with the parmesan and egg.
6. Remove browned beef to a soufflé dish that fits into your Instant Pot.
7. Add the marinara sauce to the browned meat and reserve half of the meat sauce.
8. Top the remaining meat sauce with half the mozzarella cheese.
9. Spread half the ricotta cheese mix on top of the mozzarella layer.
10. Top with the remaining meat sauce.
11. Add a layer of mozzarella cheese on top.
12. Spread the remaining ricotta cheese mixture over the mozzarella.

13. Top with the remaining mozzarella pieces.
14. Pour the water into the pot and insert the rack. Place your souffle dish on the rack.
15. Close the lid and make sure that the pressure valve is on seal.
16. Change settings to MANUAL and choose HIGH PRESSURE.
17. Set the timer to 9 minutes.
18. Once the time is up perform quick pressure release.
19. Add any remaining cheese on the top.
20. Close the lid until cheese is melted.
21. Serve and enjoy!

Beef Spaghetti Squash

Serves: 8

Preps Time: 5 min

cooking Time: 30 min

Ingredients

- 1 medium spaghetti squash
- 1 lb ground beef
- 32 oz marinara sauce
- parmesan cheese

Direction:

1. With the sharp knife, half the spaghetti squash and remove the seeds.
2. Place the rack into your Instant Pot
3. Pour in 1 cup of water and insert both halves of the squash onto the rack.

4. Turn on your Instant Pot and select MANUAL option.
5. Close the lid and make sure that the pressure valve is on seal.
6. Change settings to MANUAL and choose HIGH PRESSURE.
7. Set the timer to 10 minutes.
8.
9. Once the time is up perform quick pressure release.
10. Change settings of the pot to SAUTE.
11. Add the ground beef and saute until browned.
12. Stir in the marinara sauce and simmer for 16 minutes.
13. Serve on cooked spaghetti squash.
14. Enjoy!

Asian Short Ribs

Serves: 4

Preps Time: 15 min

cooking Time: 110 min

Ingredients:

- 4 lbs beef short ribs, individual
- 2 tsp avocado oil

For Sauce:

- 1/2 cup beef stock
- 3 green onions, roughly chopped
- 1 lemon, juiced
- 20 drops sweetener
- 1/4 cup natural rice wine vinegar - 0 carb label
- Salt and black pepper to taste
- 5 garlic cloves, smashed
- 1/4 cup organic tamari sauce, gluten free

- 1 inch piece of ginger, quartered
- 1 tbsp sesame oil - toasted

For Garnish

- sesame seeds
- 1 handful of scallions, chopped
- 1 handful of cilantro, chopped

Direction:

1. Place all sauce ingredients into blender and blend until smooth. Set aside.
2. Turn on your Instant Pot and select SAUTE option.
3. Pour in the oil and allow to heat up.
4. Season the ribs with salt & pepper.
5. Place half of the ribs into the pot and brown from each side. Same with remaining second half of ribs.
6. Turn off the pot and place all ribs into the pot.
7. Pour in the sauce.

8. Close the lid and make sure that the pressure valve is on seal.
9. Change settings to MANUAL and choose HIGH PRESSURE.
10. Set the timer to 50 minutes.
11. Once the time is up perform slow pressure release for 15 minutes and then quick pressure release.
12. Open the pot and remove the ribs.
13. Select SAUTE setting on the pot.
14. Leave the sauce to simmer for 15 minutes.
15. In the meantime, you can prepare your cauliflower rice.
16. Once the sauce is condensed, pour the sauce into a fat skimmer to remove the fat.
17. Garnish each portion and serve with your favourite side dish.
18. Enjoy!

Hot Beef

Serves: 8

Preps Time: 15 min

cooking Time: 70 min

Ingredients:

- 5-6 lbs chuck Roast
- 1 tbsp canola Oil
- 1 pack of Italian dressing seasoning
- 16 oz pepperoncini peppers, sliced
- ½ yellow onion, sliced
- 1 cup water

Direction:

1. Turn on your Instant Pot and select SAUTE option.
2. Pour in the oil and leave to heat up.

3. Place in the meat and brown for 5-6 minutes on each side.
4. Add onions, half of the jar of pepperoncini pepper, ¼ cup pepperoncini brine, Italian seasoning mix and water.
5. Close the lid and make sure that the pressure valve is on seal.
6. Change settings to MANUAL and choose HIGH PRESSURE.
7. Set the timer to 50 minutes.
8. Once the time is up perform quick pressure release.
9. Shred the meat with two forks.
10. Drain remaining pepperoncini peppers and ad to the pot.
11. Serve with your favourite side dish.
12. Enjoy!

Russian Beef Brocceto

Serves: 4

Preps Time: 5 min

cooking Time: 20 min

Ingredients:

- 2 lb flank steak, ¼ in strips
- 1 tbsp vegetable oil
- 4 cloves garlic, minced
- 1/2 cup soy sauce
- 1/2 cup water
- 2/3 cup dark brown sugar
- 1/2 tsp fresh ginger, minced
- 2 tbsp cornstarch
- 3 tbsp water
- 3 green onions, sliced

Direction:

1. Turn on your Instant Pot and select SAUTE option.
2. Pour in the oil and allow to heat up.
3. Meanwhile season the beef with salt and pepper.
4. Place the meat into the pot and brown for few minutes from each side.
5. Take the beef out and set aside.
6. Add the garlic and sauté 1 minute.
7. Add soy sauce, 1/2 cup water, brown sugar, and ginger.
8. Stir well to combine.
9. Add browned beef together with any accumulated juices.
10. Close the lid and make sure that the pressure valve is on seal.
11. Change settings to MANUAL and choose HIGH PRESSURE.
12. Set the timer to 12 minutes.

13. Once the time is up perform quick pressure release.
14. Combine the cornstarch with 3 tbsp water. Whisk until smooth.
15. Pour the cornstarch mixture into the sauce in the pot.
16. Make sure you are stirring sauce constantly.
17. Select SAUTE option and bring to a boil, stirring constantly until sauce thickens.
18. Stir in green onions.
19. Serve with your favourite side dish.
20. Enjoy!

Easy Beef Ribs

Serves: 6

Preps Time: 10 min

Cooking Time: 65 min

Ingredients:

- 2 lbs beef short ribs, bone-in
- 2 tbsp pure tallow
- 1/2 cup dry red wine
- 3 cloves garlic, sliced
- salt and pepper to taste

Direction:

1. Turn on your Instant Pot and select SAUTE option.
2. Add tallow and allow to heat up.
3. Meanwhile season the meat with salt and pepper.

4. Brown the ribs from all sides in batches. Once all meat is browned, return back to the pot.
5. Pour in the red wine.
6. Add garlic, and a little bit of salt and pepper.
7. Close the lid and make sure that the pressure valve is on seal.
8. Change settings to MANUAL and choose HIGH PRESSURE.
9. Set the timer to 50 minutes.
10. Place on lid and set valve to sealing. cook on high pressure for 50 minutes.
11. Once the time is up, perform natural pressure release.
12. Serve with your favourite side dish.
13. Enjoy!

Joe's Chunky Beef

Serves: 6

Preps Time: 15 min

cooking Time: 45 min

Ingredients:

- 2 ½ lb beef brisket, cubed
- 1 tbsp chili powder
- 1½ tsp kosher salt
- 1 tbsp coconut oil
- 1 onion, sliced
- 1 tbsp tomato paste
- 6 garlic cloves, smashed
- ½ cup tomato salsa, roasted
- ½ cup beef stock
- ½ tsp fish sauce
- black pepper to taste

For Garnish

- ½ cup cilantro, minced
- 2 radishes, thinly sliced

Direction:

1. Turn on your Instant Pot and select SAUTE option.
2. Pour in the coconut oil and allow to heat up.
3. In a separate bowl, mix together cubed beef, chili powder, and salt. Set aside.
4. Add the onions and saute for 2 minutes.
5. Stir in the garlic and tomato paste.
6. Continue to saute for 40 seconds.
7. Add marinated beef into the pot.
8. Pour in the salsa, stock, and fish sauce.
9. Close the lid and make sure that the pressure valve is on seal.
10. Change settings to MANUAL and choose HIGH PRESSURE.
11. Set the timer to 35 minutes.

12. Once the time is up perform natural pressure release.
13. Open the lid and season if required.
14. Garnish with citriano and radishes.
15. Serve with your favourite side dish.
16. Enjoy!

Simple Italian Meatballs

Serves: 4

Preps Time: 15 min

cooking Time: 20 min

Ingredients:

- 1.5 lbs ground beef
- 2 tbsp fresh parsley, chopped
- ¾ cup parmesan cheese, grated
- ½ cup almond flour
- 2 egg
- 1 tsp kosher salt
- ¼ tsp black pepper, grounded
- ¼ tsp garlic powder
- 1 tsp onion flakes, dried
- ¼ tsp oregano, dried
- 1/3 cup water, warm

- 1 tsp olive oil
- 3 cups marinara sauce, sugar free

Direction:

1. Turn on your Instant Pot and select SAUTE option.
2. In a separate bowl combine together all ingredients apart of olive oil and marinara sauce.
3. Make about 16 small meatballs from the mixture.
4. Form into approximately 16 two inch meatballs.
5. Pour in the oil and allow to heat up.
6. Saute the meatballs until browned all around.
7. Layer browned meatballs into the pot, leaving 1/2 inch of space between them.
8. Pour the marinara sauce over the meatballs.

9. Close the lid and make sure that the pressure valve is on seal.
10. Change settings to MANUAL and choose LOW PRESSURE.
11. Set the timer to 10 minutes.
12. Once the time is up perform natural pressure release.
13. Serve with your favourite side dish such as spaghetti squash.
14. Enjoy!

Creamy Beef Stroganoff

Serves: 4

Preps Time: 5 min

cooking Time: 30 min

Ingredients:

- 1 tbsp oil
- 1/2 cup onions, diced
- 1 tbsp garlic, crushed
- 1 lb beef stew meat
- 1.5 cup mushrooms, chopped
- 1 tbsp Worcestershire sauce
- 1 tsp salt
- 1/2 tsp pepper
- 3/4 cup water
- 1/3 cup sour cream
- 1/4 tsp cornstarch

Direction:

1. Turn on your Instant Pot and select SAUTE option.
2. Pour in the oil and allow to heat up.
3. Add onions and garlic. Stir.
4. Add all remaining ingredients apart of sour cream.
5. Close the lid and make sure that the pressure valve is on seal.
6. Change settings to MANUAL and choose HIGH PRESSURE.
7. Set the timer to 20 minutes.
8. Once the time is up perform natural pressure release.
9. Open the lid and change the settings back to SAUTE.
10. Add sour cream into the pot and stir well.
11. Mix the cornstarch with little bit of water.

12. Pour the mixture into the pot and saute until you will get desired thickness. Keep stirring.
13. Serve with your favourite side dish such us cauliflower rice or low carb noodles.
14. Enjoy!

Sunday Roast

Serves: 8

Preps Time: 15 min

Cooking Time: 90 min

Ingredients:

- 2 tbsp olive oil, divided
- 3 lb chuck roast meat
- 1 yellow onion, large chunks
- 3 cloves garlic, minced
- 5 carrots, medium pieces
- 15 baby potatoes, halved
- 2 tsp dried parsley
- 1 tsp dried basil
- 1 bay leaf
- 1/2 cup red wine
- 1 1/2 cups beef stock
- Salt and black pepper to taste

For gravy

- 3 tbsp butter, grass-fed
- 3 tbsp cassava Flour
- Liquid from the Instant Pot amount will vary
- Salt to taste
- Ground Black Pepper to taste

Direction:

1. Season both sides of the roast with salt and pepper and set aside.
2. Select the SAUTE option on your Instant Pot. Add 1 tablespoon of olive oil into the pot.
3. When the display says HOT and the oil is shimmering, add the roast and brown on each side for about 3 minutes. Remove the roast and set aside.
4. Pour the remaining oil into the Instant Pot which should be still hot.

5. Add onions and garlic. Sauté for 2 minutes. Press CANCEL button on the Instant Pot. Remove the onions and set aside.
6. Insert carrots and potatoes into the pot. Add the beef stock and red wine, basil, parsley, and bay leaf. Stir.
7. Insert prepared roast and top the meat with the sautéed onions.
8. Cover with the lid and close the pressure valve.
9. Press MANUAL button and set timer:
   70 min - 3 lb roast
   80 min - 3.5 lb roast
   90 min - 4 lb roast
10. Once the time is up, perform quick release of pressure.
11. Switch your Instant Pot off. Remove the roast and let rest while you make the gravy.

12. Remove the veggies with a slotted spoon.

Gravy

1. In a saucepan, melt the butter over medium-low heat.
2. Whisk in the cassava flour until you get a thin roux.
3. Add the liquid from the Instant Pot. 1/4 cup at a time, whisking and letting it gently simmer to thicken.
4. Continue until you get preferred thickness of your gravy.
5. Season with salt and pepper.

Delicious Beef Stew

Serves: 8

Preps Time: 15 min

Cooking Time: 120 min

Ingredients:

2 lbs grass-fed beef, cubed

2 tbsp coconut oil

4 cloves garlic, minced

1 medium onion, diced

1/4 cup red wine, dry

1 lb carrots, medium chunks

4 stalks celery, medium chunks

4 potatoes, large cubes

2 cups beef stock

2 tbsp Dijon mustard

2 tbsp coconut aminos

1/2 tbsp coconut palm sugar

1 tbsp rosemary, dried

1 tsp oregano, dried

1 tsp thyme, dried

¼ cup arrowroot flour

Salt and black pepper to taste

Direction:

1. Turn on your Instant Pot and select SAUTE setting.
2. Pour in the coconut oil.
3. Add the garlic, onion and rosemary.
4. Saute until until softened and fragrant.
5. Add the wine and braise the vegetables for several minutes.
6. In the separate bowl, mix together the mustard, coconut aminos, palm sugar, thyme, bay leaf, salt, pepper and the stock.
7. Add meat into your Instant Pot, and top it with the carrots, celery, and potatoes.

8. Pour over prepared mixture of stock and other ingredients.
9. Close the lid and change setting from SAUTE to MEAT/STEW.
10. Timing should be set to 35 minutes.
11. Instant Post will take about 25 minutes to pressurize.
12. Once the time is up, perform natural pressure release.
13. Ladle 1/3 cup of the cooking liquid into a bowl and whisk in the arrowroot flour. Pour the mixture into the pot and stir until you get desired thickness.
14. Serve and enjoy!

Poultry Recipes

Rustic Lemon Chicken

Serves: 6

Preps Time: 15 min

Cooking Time: 35 min

Ingredients:

- 1 whole chicken
- 1 lemon, quartered
- 2 tbsp olive oil
- 1 tsp salt
- 1 tsp garlic powder
- 1 tsp paprika
- 1/2 tsp black pepper
- 1 cup chicken stock

Direction:

1. Rinse your chicken under cold water and pat dry.

2. Insert lemon wedges inside chicken cavity and set aside.
3. Press SAUTE button on your Instant Pot.
4. In separate bowl,mix together olive oil, salt, garlic powder, paprika, and pepper.
5. Rub half of the mixture over the top side of the chicken.
6. Insert the chicken inside the pot and cook fo r4 minutes.
7. Turn the chicken over, rub remaining mixture to the bottom side of the chicken and cook for 1 more minute.
8. Remove the chicken and insert the trivet inside the pot; place the chicken back in the pot, and pour in the chicken stock.
9. Close and secure the lid.
10. Select HIGH PRESSURE and set timer for 20 minutes.
11. Allow pressure to build up, which should take about 10 min.

12. Once finished, use natural-release of pressure according to manufacturer's instructions.
13. Enjoy!

Chicken and Chorizo

Serves: 4

Preps Time: 15 min

Cooking Time: 50 min

Ingredients:

- 3 tbsp avocado oil
- 4 chicken thighs, bone-in
- 1 onion, sliced
- 4 garlic cloves, minced
- 5 thyme sprigs, leaves removed and stems discarded
- ½ lb chorizo 230 g, without casing
- 1/3 cup sun-dried tomatoes
- ½ cup green olives, pitted
- 1/3 cup orange juice
- ¾ cup chicken stock
- salt and black pepper to taste

- fresh cilantro for garnish

Direction:

1. Turn on your Instant Pot and ad 2 tbsp of avocado oil.
2. Choose SAUTE setting and leave for couple of minutes until oil heats up.
3. Add the chicken thighs, and season with salt and pepper.
4. Brown the meat for about 3 minutes on each side.
5. Once browned remove the chicken and set aside.
6. Pour 1 tbsp of avocado oil into your Instant Pot.
7. Add onion, garlic, thyme leaves and pinch of salt.
8. Saute for 5 minutes, stirring occasionally.
9. Add the chorizo and continue to sauté for another 5 minutes, stirring occasionally.

10. Choose KEEP WARM/CANCEL option on the pot.
11. Add the sun-dried tomatoes, olives, orange juice and stock. Stir well.
12. Add the chicken, and use the spoon to pour some liquid over it.
13. Cover the lid and seal the valve.
14. Change setting of the pot to POULTRY.
15. Set the timer to 20 minutes.
16. Once the time s up press KEEP WARM/CANCEL button.
17. Perform quick steam release.
18. Serve topped with fresh cilantro.
19. Enjoy!

Sobrero Chicken and Veggie Rice

Serves: 4

Preps Time: 5 min

Cooking Time: 15 min

Ingredients:

- 1 tbsp olive oil
- 1/2 cup onion, chopped
- 1 large jalapeno, chopped
- 1 tbsp minced garlic
- 1/2 tsp cumin
- 1/2 tsp chili powder
- 1/2 tsp paprika
- 1/2 tsp salt
- 2 tbsp chopped cilantro
- 4 chicken thighs, boneless
- 4 cups cauliflower, florets
- 2 tbsp. tomato paste

- 1/2 cup chicken stock

Direction:

1. Turn on your Instant Pot ad press SAUTE button.
2. Pour in the olive oil and leave it to heat up.
3. Add the onions, jalapeños, garlic, and cilantro and saute for about 1 minute.
4. Add the cumin, chili powder, paprika, salt and stir.
5. Insert your chicken thighs into the pot and pour in the stock.
6. Close the lid and seal the pressure valve.
7. Press the MANUAL button on the pot.
8. Choose HIGH PRESSURE and set the timer to 9 minutes.
9. Once the time is up perform quick release of pressure.
10. Open the lid and place a steaming basket over the chicken.

11. Add the cauliflower into the basket and close the lid again.
12. Continue cooking on HIGH PRESSURE for another minute.
13. Perform quick release of pressure and remove the basket from the pot.
14. Remove the chicken and set aside.
15. Strain the liquid
16. Return the onions and jalapenos back to the pot and add 2 tbsp of strained liquid.
17. Place the cauliflower into the pot and mush it up into small chunks with potato masher.
18. Add tomato paste and stir.
19. Serve and enjoy!

Whole Garlic Chicken

Serves: 4

Preps Time: 10 min

Cooking Time: 40 min

Ingredients:

- 1 whole chicken
- 3 cloves of garlic, minced
- 1 tbsp olive oil
- 1 medium lemon, organic - sliced
- 2 cups water
- 1 tbsp apple cider vinegar
- Salt and black pepper to taste

Direction:

1. Mix salt and pepper with olive oil and rub the mixture over your chicken.
2. Insert lemon slices in chickens cavity.

3. Turn on your Instant Pot and place the rack inside.
4. Pour in the water and apple cider vinegar.
5. Close the lid and choose POULTRY setting.
6. Set the timer to 25 minutes.
7. Once the time runs up perform natural pressure release for about 15 minutes.
8. Leave the chicken to stand for 10 minutes before carving.
9. Serve with your favourite side dish.

Moist Turkey With Gravy

Serves: 4

Preps Time: 15 min

Cooking Time: 60 min

Ingredients:

- 1 turkey breast
- 2 ribs celery, cut into large chunks
- 1 onion, large chunks
- 1 oz package onion soup mix
- 1 cup chicken stock
- 2 tbsps water
- 1 tbsp cornstarch
- Salt and black pepper to taste

Direction:

1. Turn on your Instant pot.

2. Season turkey breast with onion soup mixture and insert it into the pot.
3. Top seasoned turkey breast with celery and onion.
4. Pour in the chicken stock close the lid and seal.
5. Choose POULTRY option on your Instant pot.
6. Cook for 30 minutes. Once the time runs out pierce the breast with the fork to make sure that its cooked and juices run clear.
7. Perform natural release of the pressure which should take about 20 minutes.
8. Leave turkey to rest for 10 minutes before carving.
9. Now select SAUTE option on your Instant Pot.
10. In a separate bowl, mix together water and cornstarch.
11. Add a little bit of hot liquid from the pot.

12. Stir until dissolved.
13. Pour the mixture into the pot and whisk until you will get desired thickens.
14. Serve with your favourite side dish.
15. Enjoy!

Instant Pot Faux Pho

Serves: 6

Preps Time: 5 min

Cooking Time: 45 min

Ingredients:

- 4 lbs chicken legs, halved, bone-in, skin on
- 1 tbsp olive oil
- 2 onions, quartered
- 1 inch of ginger, peeled, roughly chopped
- 1 tbsp coriander seeds
- 1 tsp green cardamom pods
- 1 black cardamom pod
- 1 cinnamon stick
- 4 cloves garlic
- 1 lemongrass, stalk trimmed, 2 inch pieces
- 1/4 cup fish sauce

- 1 cup fresh cilantro
- 1 head bok choy, roughly chopped
- 1 large daikon, root spiralized
- Salt and pepper to taste

For Garnish

- lime wedges
- fresh basil

Direction:

1. Toast coriander seeds in a dry skillet for 5 - 6 minutes.
2. Turn on your Instant Pot and select SAUTE option.
3. Rinse the meat and pat dry.
4. Pour the oil into the pot and allow to heat up.
5. Add onion and saute for 2 minutes.
6. Add the meat and all spices. Saute for another 2 minutes

7. Add the the cilantro, lemongrass, and fish sauce.
8. Pour in enough cold water to cover.
9. Close the lid and make sure that the pressure valve is on seal.
10. Change settings to MANUAL and choose HIGH PRESSURE.
11. Set the timer to 30 minutes.
12. Once the time is up perform quick pressure release.
13. Remove the chicken and shred with the fork.
14. Strain the liquid from the pot and pour it back into the cooker.
15. Change the settings to SAUTE and add the bok choy and spiralized daikon.
16. Leave it to simmer for 5 minutes.
17. Garnish each portion with basil and lime.
18. Serve with your favourite side dish.
19. Enjoy!

Quick Citrus Chicken

Serves: 4

Preps Time: 15 min

Cooking Time: 15 min

Ingredients:

- 3 lb chicken breast, boneless, skinless, cubed
- 2 tbsp coconut oil
- 1/4 cup Chicken stock
- 4 tbsp brown sugar
- 3 tbsp ketchup
- 6 drops orange essential oil
- ¼ cup flour

Direction:

1. Turn on your Instant Pot and select SAUTE option.

2. Coat chicken cubes in the flower.
3. Add coconut oil into the pot and leave it to heat up.
4. Insert the chicken and brown it for 2 minutes stirring occasionally.
5. Change the setting of your Instant Pot to MANUAL.
6. Add the stock, sugar, ketchup and orange essential oil.
7. Close the lid, select HIGH PRESSURE and set the timer to 15 minutes.
8. Once the time is up, perform a quick release of the pressure. Stir.
9. Serve with rice.
10. Enjoy!

Hot Chicken Chili

Serves: 4

Preps Time: 15 min

Cooking Time: 25 min

Ingredients:

- 1 cup white onion, finely chopped
- 2 tbsp olive oil
- 2/3 cups jalapeño peppers, seeded, finely chopped
- 3 garlic cloves, minced
- 3 cup chicken breast, boneless, cubed
- 2 tsp chili powder
- 1 tsp cumin, graded
- 1 tsp Oregano, Dried
- 2 cup Chicken stock
- 10 oz tomatoes with green chiles, canned
- 14 oz whole kernel corn, canned

- 3 tbsp cream cheese
- 1 cup bacon, cooked, chopped
- salt and black pepper to taste

Direction:

- Turn on your Instant Pot and select Saute option.
- Pour in the oil and leave it to heat up.
- Add onions, jalapeno, garlic, chili powder, cumin, salt, black pepper, and oregano to the pot.
- Saute for for 1 minute and add chicken.
- Continue to saute for 2 minutes, stirring occasionally.
- Choose MANUAL setting on the pot.
- Close the lead and make sure that the vent is on seal.
- Select HIGH PRESSURE and set the timer to 10 minutes.

- Once the time is up perform quick pressure release.
- Press the KEEP WARM/CANCEL button and stir in the cream cheese and half of the bacon.
- Leave it to cook for for 3 minutes.
- Serve topped with the bacon and your favorite side dish.
- Enjoy!

Whole Chicken

Serves: 5

Preps Time: 5 min

Cooking Time: 40 min

Ingredients:

- 1 whole chicken, organic
- 1 tbsp Coconut Oil 1 tsp. paprika
- 1½ cup chicken stock
- 1 tsp thyme, dried
- ¼ tsp black pepper
- 2 tbsp lemon juice
- ½ tsp salt
- 6 cloves garlic, peeled

Direction:

1. In a separate bowl, mix together paprika, thyme, salt, and pepper.

2. Rub the mixture over the chicken.
3. Turn on your Instant Pot and select SAUTE option.
4. Pour in the coconut oil and allow it to heat up.
5. Place the chicken into the pot, make sure it's breast side down and brown it for 6-7 minutes.
6. Flip the bird and pour in the stock and lemon juice.
7. Add garlic cloves.
8. Close the lid and make sure that the pressure valve is on seal.
9. Change settings to MANUAL and choose HIGH PRESSURE.
10. Set the timer to 25 minutes.
11. Once the time is up perform natural pressure release.
12. Remove the chicken from the pot and let it stand for 8 minutes before carving.

13. Serve with your favourite side dish.
14. Enjoy!

Rice, Chicken and Bacon

Serves: 4

Preps Time: 15 min

Cooking Time: 20 min

Ingredients:

- 8 pieces of bacon, chopped
- 1 cup chicken stock
- 1 tsp ranch seasoning
- 2 lb chicken breasts, skinless, boneless
- 8 oz. light cream cheese, softened, cubed
- 1/2 cup monterey jack cheese, shredded
- 4 green onions, chopped

Direction:

- Turn on your Instant Pot and select SAUTE option.
- Add the bacon and saute until crisped.

- Take the bacon out and drain the grease from the pot.
- Return the bacon back to the pot and pour in the chicken stock.
- Add ranch seasoning, and chicken.
- Press the MANUAL button on your pot and close the lid.
- Choose HIGH PRESSURE and set the timer to 12 minutes.
- Once the time runs up perform slow pressure release for 5 minutes and then quick pressure release.
- Remove the meat from the pot, and shred with the fork.
- Set the pot to SAUTE option again and add cream cheese, whisking it until it's melted.
- Add shredded chicken back into the pot, and stir well to combine.
- Serve over rice topped with shredded cheese and chopped green onions.

- Enjoy!

Turkey Chili

Serves: 4

Preps Time: 15 min

Cooking Time: 200 min

Ingredients

- 1 tbsp coconut oil
- 3 cloves garlic, minced
- 2 onions, diced
- 2 red bell peppers, chopped
- 2 carrots, chopped
- 2 celery ribs, chopped
- 1 sweet potato, peeled, cubed
- 2 lb ground turkey
- 15 oz diced tomatoes
- 15 oz tomato sauce
- 6 oz tomato paste
- 2 cups water

- 1 tbsp salt
- 3 tbsp chili powder
- 1 tbsp red paprika
- 1/2 tsp cayenne pepper
- 1 tbsp ground cumin
- 2 tsp celery seed
- 1/2 tsp ground black pepper
- red pepper flakes to taste

Directions

1. Turn on your Instant Pot and select SAUTE option.
2. Pour in the oil and allow to heat up.
3. Add the garlic, onions, peppers, carrots, celery, and sweet potato.
4. Saute for 6 minutes.
5. Add the turkey meat and brown while stirring often.
6. Add the water, diced tomatoes, tomato sauce, tomato paste, salt, and all spices.

7. Stir well to combine.
8. Once the boiling point is reached, reduce the heat and simmer uncovered for 3 hours.
9. Taste and season as required.
10. Serve and enjoy!

Chicken Stew

Serves: 8

Preps Time: 15 min

Cooking Time: 25 min

Ingredients:

- 4 chicken legs, separated thigh and drumsticks
- 1 tbsp coconut oil
- 2 tbsp achiote seasoning
- 2 tbsp white vinegar
- 3 tbsp worcestershire sauce
- 1 cup yellow onion, sliced
- 3 cloves garlic, sliced
- 1 tsp cumin, grounded
- 1 tsp dried oregano
- 1/2 tsp black pepper
- 1 tbsp granulated sugar substitute

- 2 cups chicken stock

Direction:

1. In separate bowl, mix together achiote paste, vinegar, worcestershire sauce, cumin, oregano, pepper and sweetener.
2. Add chicken into the mixture and marinade for 1 hour.
3. Turn on your Instant Pot and select SAUTE option.
4. Pour in the coconut oil and leave it to heat up.
5. Add marinated chicken pieces and brown the meat for about 3 minutes.
6. Keep the marinade aside.
7. Remove the browned chicken and set asside.
8. Add the onions and garlic into the Instant Pot and saute for 2 minutes.

9. Insert your browned meat back into the pot.
10. Mix the marinade with chicken stock.
11. Pour the mixture over the chicken.
12. Set the pot to MANUAL and close the lid. Make sure that the vent is on seal position.
13. Choose HIGH PRESSURE and set the timer to 20 minutes.
14. Once the time runs up perform quick release of the steam.
15. Serve and enjoy!

Tender Mediterranean Chicken

Serves: 4

Preps Time: 5 min

Cooking Time: 40 min

Ingredients:

- 1 whole chicken
- 1 tbsp olive oil
- 1/2 cup water
- 1 tbsp lemon juice
- 2 tsp rosemary, dried
- 1 tsp thyme, dried
- 1 tsp salt
- 1/2 tsp black pepper
- 1 whole bayleaf

Direction:

1. Turn on your Instant Pot and choose SAUTE setting.

2. Pour olive oil into the pot and leave it to heat up.
3. Meanwhile rub the chicken with herbs and season according to taste.
4. Insert the chicken in the pot, breast side up first
5. Brown the chicken skin for 4 minutes on each side.
6. Remove browned chicken and insert the rack into the pot.
7. Place chicken on the rack, and pour 1/2 cup water and lemon juice over your browned chicken.
8. Close the lid and choose POULTRY option on your pot.
9. Set the timer to 27 minutes.
10. Once the time is up perform natural pressure release and open the lid.
11. Serve with your favourite side dish.
12. Enjoy!

Sunday Turkey Breast

Serves: 2

Preps Time: 10 min

Cooking Time: 9 min

Ingredients:

- 1 cup water
- 2 turkey breast fillets
- 1 tbsp garlic powder
- 1 tbsp rosemary
- 1 tbsp sage
- 1/2 tsp thyme
- salt and pepper to taste

Direction:

1. Turn on your Instant Pot and place inside the rack.

2. Rub the turkey breasts with herbs and spices.
3. Insert the meat into the pot and cover the lid.
4. Choose POULTRY option and set the timer to 8 minutes.
5. Once the time is up, perform a quick pressure release and remove the turkey breasts from the pot.
6. Serve the liquid alongside of the meat and your favourite side dish.
7. Enjoy!

Green Chicken Chili

Serves: 4

Preps Time: 5 min

Cooking Time: 30 min

Ingredients:

- 3 lb chicken thighs and drumsticks, bone-in, skin-on
- 3/4 lb tomatillos, quartered
- 3 poblano peppers, roughly chopped, seeded
- 2 Anaheim peppers, roughly chopped, seeded
- 2 jalapeno peppers, roughly chopped
- 1 white onion, roughly chopped
- 6 medium cloves garlic, peeled
- 1 tbsp cumin, grounded
- 1/2 cup fresh cilantro leaves

- 1 tbsp Asian fish sauce
- corn tortillas
- 4 lime wedges
- salt to taste

Direction:

1. Turn on your Instant pot and select SAUTE option.
2. Add chicken, tomatillos, poblano peppers, Anaheim peppers, onion, garlic, cumin, and salt into the pot.
3. Saute for 3 - 4 minutes, stirring occasionally.
4. Close the lid and press the MANUAL button on the pot.
5. Choose HIGH PRESSURE and set the timer to 15 minutes
6. Once the time is up perform quick pressure release.

7. Take the chicken out of the pot and set aside.
8. Add cilantro, fish sauce and remaining contents of Instant Pot to a blender and blend well. Taste the sauce and season if necessary.
9. Take chicken out of the bone and shred.
10. Return shredded chicken back to the sauce.
11. Serve on the tortillas with slice of lime or citriano.
12. Enjoy!

Pork Recipes

Easy Jamaican Jerk

Serves: 10

Preps Time: 5 min

Cooking Time: 50 min

Ingredients:

- 4 lb pork shoulder
- 1/4 cup Jamaican Jerk spice blend
- 1 tbsp olive oil
- 1/2 cup beef stock

Direction:

1. In the separate bowl, mix together olive oil and Jamaican Jerk spice blend.
2. Rub the mixture over pork shoulder.
3. Turn on your Instant Pot and select SAUTE option.

4. Brown the meat from each side for 2 minutes.
5. Add the stock and close the lid.
6. Switch to MANUAL setting and select HIGH PRESSURE.
7. Set the timer to 45 minutes.
8. Once the time is up perform quick pressure release.
9. Shred the meat and serve with your favourite side dish.
10. Enjoy!

Roasted Pork and Mushrooms

Serves: 4

Preps Time: 15 min

Cooking Time: 70 min

Ingredients:

- 3 lb pork roast
- 1 tsp salt
- ½ tsp black pepper
- 4 cups cauliflower, chopped
- 1 white onion, coarsely chopped
- 4 cloves garlic
- 2 celery ribs
- 8 oz portabella mushrooms, sliced
- 2 tbsp organic coconut oil
- 2 cups water

Direction:

1. Turn on your Instant Pot and set on MANUAL setting.
2. Insert cauliflower, onion, garlic, celery and pour the water into pot.
3. Season the meat with salt and pepper and place into the pot.
4. Choose HIGH PRESSURE and set the timer to 60 minutes.
5. Once the time is up perform quick pressure release.
6. Meanwhile preheat the oven to 400 F.
7. Remove the pork roast from the Instant Pot and place in an oven proof dish.
8. Place the meat into the owen and bake for 15 minutes.
9. Blend all vegetables and liquid together in the blender until smooth. Set aside.
10. Switch your Instant Pot to SAUTE setting and add mushrooms and coconut oil.

11. Saute for about 4 minutes until soft.
12. Add blended mixture and continue to saute until your gravy reaches desired thickness.
13. Serve the meat with mushroom gravy and your favourite side dish.
14. Enjoy!

Haway Pork Deli

Serves: 8

Preps Time: 5 min

Cooking Time: 100 min

Ingredients:

- 5 lb pork shoulder, bone-in
- 1 tsp salt
- 1/2 cup pineapple, diced
- 1 tsp fish sauce
- 1 tbsp liquid smoke
- 1/2 cup water

Direction:

1. Turn on your Instant Pot and press the MANUAL button.
2. Season the meat and place it into the pot.

3. Add the pineapple, fish sauce, liquid smoke and water.
4. Close the lid and make sure that the valve is set to seal.
5. Choose HIGH PRESSURE and set the timer to 90 minutes.
6. Once the time runs up, perform natural pressure release for 15 minutes and then use Quick Pressure Release.
7. Remove the meat from the pot shred with the fork. Remove excess fat.
8. Pour the juices into separate bowl and wait until fat raises into the top.
9. Remove the fat from the top of the liquid and discard.
10. Pour half of the liquid into shredded meat.
11. Serve with your favourite side dish.
12. Enjoy!

Simple Pork chops

Serves: 4

Preps Time: 5 min

cooking Time: 5 min

Ingredients:

- 1 tbsp of coconut oil
- 4-6 pork chops, boneless
- 1 stick of butter
- 1 package of ranch mix
- 1 cup of chicken stock

Direction:

1. Turn on your Instant Pot and select SAUTE option.
2. Pour in the coconut oil and allow to heat up. Place the meat into the pot and brown from both sides.

3. Once browned place the butter on the top of the pork and season with ranch mix seasoning.
4. Pour the chicken stock over the pork.
5. Close the lid and make sure that the pressure valve is on seal.
6. Change settings to MANUAL and choose HIGH PRESSURE.
7. Set the timer to 5 minutes.
8. Once the time is up, perform slow pressure release for 5 minutes and then quick pressure release.
9. Serve with your favourite side dish.
10. Enjoy!

Italian Sausage Mix

Serves: 3

Preps Time: 15 min

cooking Time: 25 min

Ingredients:

- 38 oz packages Pork Italian Sausages such as Johnsonville
- 4 green bell peppers, seeded, 1/2 inch strips
- 28 oz diced tomatoes
- 15 oz tomato sauce
- 1 cup water
- 1 tbsp basil, dried
- 4 cloves garlic, minced
- 1 tbsp Italian seasoning

Direction:

1. Turn on your Instant Pot.
2. Add tomatoes, tomato sauce, water, basil, garlic powder and Italian seasoning and stir to combine.
3. Add sausages and top with the peppers. Do not stir.
4. Close the lid and make sure that the pressure valve is on seal.
5. Change settings to MANUAL and choose HIGH PRESSURE.
6. Set the timer to 25 minutes.
7. Once the time is up perform quick pressure release.
8. Open the lid and serve with your favourite side dish.
9. Enjoy!

Home Made Ribs

Serves: 6

Preps Time: 15 min

Cooking Time: 20 min

Ingredients:

- 2.5 lb country pork ribs, boneless - cubed
- 2 tbsp sesame oil
- 4 garlic cloves, minced
- ¼ tsp turmeric
- 1 cup beef stock
- ⅛ cup fresh ginger, grated
- Salt and black pepper to taste

Direction:

1. To create marinade, add oil, garlic, tumeric, ginger, salt and pepper to medium bowl. Stir to combine.

2. Add cubed ribs and mix it well.
3. Cover with cling film and place in the fridge for at least 30 minutes to marinade.
4. Turn on your Instant Pot and choose SAUTE option.
5. Place marinated pork into the pot and brown it for 5 minutes.
6. Add beef stock and stir it well.
7. Cover the lid and set the vent to SEAL position.
8. Set the timer to 17 minutes and choose the HIGH PRESSURE High Pressure.
9. Once the time runs up perform quick pressure release.
10. Serve with your favourite side dish.
11. Enjoy!

Pulled Pork Burrito

Serves: 4

Preps Time: 5 min

Cooking Time: 60 min

Ingredients:

- 2 1/2 lb pork shoulder roast, boneless, quartered
- 6 cloves garlic, quartered
- 2 tbsp sesame oil
- 1 1/2 tsp cumin
- 1/2 tsp sazon
- 1/4 tsp dry oregano
- 1 cup chicken stock, reduced sodium
- 2 chipotle peppers in adobo sauce
- 2 bay leaves
- 1/4 tsp adobo seasoning, dry
- 1/2 tsp garlic powder

- 2 tsp salt
- black pepper, to taste
- burritos

Direction:

1. Turn on your Instant Pot and select SAUTE option.
2. In separate bowl, mix together oil, salt and pepper. Rub the mixture over the pork meat.
3. Brown the pork on each side for 4 minutes.
4. Remove the meat from the pot and allow to cool.
5. Pierce the pork evenly with the sharp knife, making 1-inch deep holes, and insert the garlic into each hole.
6. Season the meat with cumin, sazon, oregano, adobo and garlic powder.
7. Pour chicken stock into your Instant Pot.

8. Add chipotle peppers, bay leaves and stir.
9. Place the pork inside and cover the lid.
10. Set your pot to MANUAL and HIGH PRESSURE.
11. Set the timer to 80 minutes.
12. Perform natural pressure release and open the lid.
13. Shred the pork and stir well to combine with juices.
14. Remove bay leaves and add adobo. Stir.
15. Serve on burritos.
16. Enjoy!

Curry Recipes

Quick Lamb curry

Serves: 4

Preps Time: 10 min

cooking Time: 50 min

Ingredients:

- 2 tbsp avocado oil
- 2 lb lamb shoulder, bone-in
- 2 onions, diced
- 1 ½ inch fresh ginger, minced
- 3 cloves garlic, minced
- 4 cloves garlic, whole
- 4 cardamom pods
- 1 bay leaf
- 1 tbsp coriander powder
- 1 tsp ground cumin
- 1 tsp garam masala
- 1 tsp paprika

- 1 tsp turmeric
- ¼ tsp cayenne
- 14 oz can organic diced tomatoes
- ½ cup water
- ½ lb potatoes, halved
- salt to taste

Direction:

1. Turn on your Instant Pot and select SAUTE option.
2. Pour in the oil and allow it to heat up.
3. Brown the meat for 2 minutes, stirring occasionally.
4. Add the onion, garlic, ginger and all spices.
5. Saute for 2-3 minutes.
6. Add diced tomatoes, water and potatoes. Stir.
7. Close the lid and make sure that the pressure valve is on seal.

8. Change settings to MANUAL and choose HIGH PRESSURE.
9. Set the timer to 45 minutes.
10. Once the time is up perform natural pressure release.
11. Change the settings to SAUTE again and reduce liquid until your curry reaches desired consistency.
12. Serve with your favourite side dish.
13. Garnish and enjoy!

Indian Keema Curry

Serves: 4

Preps Time: 10 min

Cooking Time: 20 min

Ingredients:

- 2 tbsp ghee
- 1 onion, finely diced
- 4 tsp garlic, minced
- 1 tsp ginger, minced
- 1 green chili, minced
- 1 tbsp coriander powder
- 1 tsp paprika
- 1 tsp salt
- ½ tsp black pepper
- ½ tsp ground cumin
- ½ tsp garam masala
- ½ tsp turmeric

- ¼ tsp cayenne
- ¼ tsp ground cardamom
- 1 lb ground meat of your choice
- 14.5 oz diced tomatoes, canned
- 2 cup peas
- Cilantro, garnish

Direction:

1. Turn on your Instant Pot and select SAUTE option.
2. Add the ghee and onions.
3. Saute for 8-10 minutes.
4. Add the garlic, ginger, green chilli and al spices to the pot.
5. Continue to saute for 30 seconds
6. Add the meat and saute for 5 minutes.
7. Add the diced tomatoes and peas. Stir well
8. Close the lid and make sure that the pressure valve is on seal.

9. Change settings to MANUAL and choose HIGH PRESSURE.
10. Set the timer to 10 minutes.
11. Once the time is up perform quick pressure release.
12. Press the SAUTE button again and reduce liquid until you will reach desired consistency.
13. Serve with citriano as a garnish.
14. Enjoy!

Caribbean Curry

Serves: 4

Preps Time: 10 min

Cooking Time: 20 min

Ingredients:

- 2.8 lb chicken thighs
- 1 tsp curry powder
- 4 tbsp avocado oil
- 1 onion, finely sliced
- 1 tbsp garlic, minced
- 2 sprigs of thyme
- 1 tsp paprika
- 1 cup coconut milk
- 1/2 cup chicken stock
- 1 bay leaf
- 1 tbsp tomato paste
- 1 scotch bonnet pepper

- 1 lb potatoes, peeled, cubed
- 1 lb carrots
- salt and pepper to taste

Direction:

1. In separate bowl, marinade chicken in salt, pepper and half of prepared curry spice. Set aside
2. Turn on your Instant Pot and select SAUTE option.
3. Pour in 2 tbsp of oil and allow to heat up.
4. Brown the chicken for about 3 minutes for each side.
5. Remove browned chicken and set aside.
6. Drain the pot and add 2 tbsp of fresh oil.
7. Add onions, garlic, thyme, paprika, curry powder.
8. Saute for 5 minutes, stirring occasionally.
9. Add scotch bonnet, coconut milk, water, bay leaf and tomato paste.

10. Continue to saute for another 2 minutes.
11. Season with salt pepper and chicken bouillon.
12. Add chicken and stir to combine.
13. Close the lid and make sure that the pressure valve is on seal.
14. Change settings to MANUAL and choose HIGH PRESSURE.
15. Set the timer to 10 minutes.
16. Once the time is up perform quick pressure release.
17. Change settings of your pot to Saute.
18. Add potatoes and all vegetables.
19. Bring to boil and continue to saute until potatoes and veg are soft.
20. Serve with your favourite side dish.
21. Enjoy!

Sushmas Beef Curry

Serves: 4

Preps Time: 15 min

cooking Time: 40 min

Ingredients:

- 1 lb beef stew chunks, grass-fed
- 2 tbsp coconut oil
- 1 onion, diced
- 3 sweet potatoes, cubed
- 6 carrots, cubed
- 5 cloves garlic, diced
- 1 cup coconut milk
- 1/2 cup vegetable stock
- 1 1/2 tbsp curry powder
- 1 tsp sea salt
- 1/2 tsp black pepper
- 1 tsp oregano, dried

- 1/4 tsp paprika

Direction:

1. Turn on your Instant Pot and select SAUTE option.
2. Pour in the oil and allow to heat up.
3. Add the onion and garlic.
4. Saute for two minutes, stirring occasionally.
5. Add the meat and brown it from each side for about 5 minutes.
6. Add the remaining ingredients and stir well to combine.
7. Close the lid and make sure that the pressure valve is on seal.
8. Change settings to MEAT/STEW.
9. Set the timer to 30 minutes.
10. Once the time is up perform quick pressure release.

11. Serve with cauliflower rice or your favourite side dish.
12. Enjoy!

Chinese Curry

Serves: 4

Preps Time: 10 min

cooking Time: min

Ingredients:

- 1 lb chicken thighs
- 1 lb chicken drumsticks
- 1 tbsp madras curry
- 1 tsp onion powder
- 1 tsp garlic powder
- salt and black pepper to taste
- 1 onion, chopped
- 4 garlic cloves, minced
- 2 stalks of lemongrass, 2 inch pieces
- 1 tbsp ginger, minced
- 2 tbsp fish sauce
- 1 tbsp sugar

- 3 tbsp madras curry
- 1 cup chicken stock
- 1 can coconut milk
- 3 carrots, medium cubes
- 4 yukon gold potatoes, medium cubes

Direction:

1. In separate bowl, mix together 1 tbsp madras curry, onion powder, garlic powder, and salt.
2. Add the chicken and leave to marinade for 15 minutes.
3. Turn on your Instant Pot and select SAUTE option.
4. Pour in the oil and allow to heat up.
5. Add onions and saute for 2 minutes.
6. Add meat, ginger and garlic. Saute for another 30 seconds.
7. Add all of remaining ingredients but only half of the coconut milk.

8. Close the lid and make sure that the pressure valve is on seal.
9. Change settings of your pot to MEAT/STEW and set the timer to 10 minutes.
10. Once the time is up perform quick pressure release.
11. Open the lid and add remaining coconut milk.
12. Season to taste.
13. Serve with your favourite side dish.
14. Enjoy!

Citrus and Coconut Curry

Serves: 4

Preps Time: 10 min

cooking Time: 30 min

Ingredients:

- 1 1/2 chicken breasts
- 1/4 tsp sea salt
- 1/4 tsp black pepper
- 1 tbsp coconut oil
- 1/2 cup red onion, finely chopped
- 1 red chili, chopped
- 1 cup chicken stock
- 2 tbsp fresh lime juice
- 1 tbsp cilantro, chopped
- 1/2 tsp red chili flakes
- 1/2 cup full fat coconut milk
- 1 tsp turmeric powder

- 1 tbsp cornstarch

Direction:

1. Turn on your Instant Pot and select SAUTE option.
2. Pour in the coconut oil and allow to heat up.
3. Add the red onions and saute for 3 minutes.
4. Add the chicken stock, lime juice, red pepper flakes, coconut milk and turmeric. Season with salt and pepper.
5. Simmer for 40 seconds stirring occasionally.
6. Add the chicken and stir to combine.
7. Close the lid and make sure that the pressure valve is on seal.
8. Change settings to MANUAL and choose HIGH PRESSURE.
9. Set the timer to 8 minutes.

10. Once the time is up perform natural pressure release for 10 minutes and then quick pressure release.
11. Remove the chicken and cube with sharp knife.
12. Change settings to SAUTE.
13. Bring sauce to boil and mix cornstarch with a little bit of water.
14. Saute for 2 minutes.
15. Add cubed chicken and chopped citriano.
16. Simer for 30 seconds and press the CANCEL button.
17. Taste and season with salt and pepper if required.
18. Serve with your favourite side dish.
19. Enjoy!

Keto Tikka Masala

Serves: 4

Preps Time: 10 min

cooking Time: min

Ingredients:

- 1 tbsp ghee
- 1 tbsp coconut oil
- 1 onion, diced
- 1 tbsp garam masala
- 2 tsp salt
- 1 tsp cumin
- 1 tsp turmeric
- 1 tsp ground coriander
- 1 tsp chili powder
- 1/2 tsp black pepper
- 6 cloves garlic, diced
- 2 inch knob of ginger, peeled, diced

- 24 oz organic tomatoes, diced
- 1-1/2 lb chicken breasts, boneless, skinless
- 3 tbsp coconut milk
- 2 tbsp almond butter

Direction:

1. Turn on your Instant Pot and select SAUTE option.
2. Add the ghee and allow to heat up.
3. Add the onion and saute for 4 minutes.
4. Add all of the spices and stir to combine.
5. Saute for 1 minute.
6. Add the garlic, ginger, and diced tomatoes.
7. Saute for 30 seconds. Stir well.
8. Add chicken breast and mix to combine.
9. Close the lid and make sure that the pressure valve is on seal.
10. Change settings to MANUAL and choose HIGH PRESSURE.

11. Set the timer to 16 minutes.
12. Once the time is up perform quick pressure release.
13. Remove the chicken and shred with 2 forks and set aside.
14. Stir in the almond butter and coconut milk in the sauce.
15. Blend the sauce in the blender until nice and smooth.
16. Add the shredded chicken.
17. Serve with your favourite side dish.
18. Enjoy!

Made in the USA
Las Vegas, NV
28 November 2021

35519594R00108